Cookbook for a Man

---

whose wife no longer likes to cook!

"Classic Italian Favorites"

"Let's Get Cooking!"

ROY BAIN

Available as ebook

ISBN 979-8-9919072-2-4 (Paperback)

The Library of Congress has cataloged this edition as follows:

Cookbook for a Man Whose Wife No longer Likes to Cook Roy Bain

Printed in the United States of America. Published by

I **Q** InfoQuest, San Diego, California

The reason I wrote this book!

"Most men love to eat a well-cooked meal, however. . .

. . . their loving wife is all-cooked-out!"

Problem is: Most men don't know how to boil water!

The good news is. . .
"You don't have to know how to cook everything."

It is my pleasure to welcome you to this collection of classic Italian favorites. My mission is to present a dozen easy to cook recipes that almost any man can follow to create a great meal. I am eighty-six-years-old, and I spent a lot of time searching for something good to eat that was EASY to cook. I usually started with a basic recipe and added ingredients I like. Some meals I cooked were just okay, others were a little better, and a few were great! I kept the "easy to cook" great ones, and they are included in this book. These recipes are fun to cook, and they are delicious! My younger brother, Don, told me he has been eating peanut butter and jelly sandwiches for dinner because his wife no longer cooks. If you just learn to cook this dozen recipes, you can enjoy eating well again! Your wife will like them too. You will love these meals and maybe your wife will help you get started. She will be happy and love you for it.

Maybe you will want to cook dinner for a few friends. This is a little poem I wrote to express my feelings about friends:

Friends ❤️

Shine a lot of love on your friends and quickly you will learn.
The more love you give to others, the more they'll give you in return.
Be a giver that's what matters, reach out and help a friend.
It's the hand that gives that gathers; you'll be the winner in the end.
Cast your love upon the water, it was never meant to keep.
Give of yourself a little harder for as ye sow, so shall ye reap.
So, shine a lot of love on your friends, and you'll find as you do.
The more love you shine upon them, the more love they'll shine on you!

What's for Dinner?

Choose your favorite:

1. "Penne and Meatballs From Heaven"
2. 🐔 Chicken with Brandy
3. Chicken Scallopini 🐔
4. "Haley's Favorite" Italian Casserole
5. Italian Pesto for Lovers
6. "Grandpa Roy's" Linguini Alla Vongole
7. "Heavenly" Chicken Alfredo 🐔
8. 🐔 Champagne Chicken
9. "See You in My Dreams" Fettuccine 🐔
10. 🔥 "Serve Me Hot" Rigatoni
11. "Million Dollar" Baked Ziti
12. Garlic Goddess Pasta

A little something on the side:

"Crazy-good" 🔥 Garlic Kiscuits

"Home-made" Happy Buns

"Honey Glazed" Carrots 🥕

"Tender Sweet" Baby Beets

Something sweet to eat:

Strawberry Delight 🍓

"Blow your Mind" Cherries Jubilee 🍒

Guide to measures:

oz = ounce   t = teaspoon

lb. = pound   T = Tablespoon

c = cup

Penne and Meatballs From Heaven

30 minutes　　　　**4 servings**

Directions:

In a large skillet over medium heat, sauté the beef in small pieces until redness is gone, about 7-8 minutes. In a separate covered pan with olive oil, sauté the onion, green and red peppers, until tender. Add garlic and cook for one more minute. Cook meatballs as recipe instructs. Boil pasta until al dente. Remove grease from ground beef. Add sauce to ground beef over low heat. Add pasta to sauce and mix. Add onions and peppers to mix and then top with meatballs. Sprinkle with Parmesan cheese. Serve hot!

INGREDIENTS:

8 oz.	Penne pasta
½	Green bell pepper, sliced into ½ inch strips
½	Red bell pepper, sliced into ½ inch strips
½	Onion, sliced into ½ inch strips
2 T	Garlic, minced
½ lb.	Ground beef
1 lb.	Italian Meatballs
1 jar	Pasta sauce (Classico Italian Sausage)
2 T	Olive oil
	Salt, pepper to taste
	Parmesan cheese to taste, grated

Haley and good friend, Taylor

Chicken with Brandy

30 minutes   4 servings

Directions:

Heat vegetable oil and 1 tablespoon of butter on medium-high in a large skillet. Season chicken with salt and pepper, then place in skillet. Sauté

chicken until each side is browned, about 5 minutes per side. Transfer chicken to a plate. With skillet still at medium-high, add remaining butter and mushrooms, sauté until brown, about 5-6 minutes. Cook fettuccine until al dente. Add shallot and cook until tender, about 3 minutes. Add the brandy and leave unstirred for 20 seconds. Add broth, heavy cream, lemon juice, mustard, garlic, and Worcestershire sauce to mushroom mixture and cook for about 3 minutes. Add fettuccine. Add salt and pepper to taste and stir in parsley. Return chicken to mix. Add lemon slices and serve.

Great with pasta

INGREDIENTS:

4	Boneless and skinless medium sized chicken breasts
1½ t	Kosher salt
1 t	Black pepper
1 T	Vegetable oil
2 T	Unsalted butter
2-8 oz	Packages of fresh sliced button mushrooms
1 lg	Shallot, finely chopped.
2 T	Brandy
½ c	Chicken broth
½ c	Heavy whipping cream
3 T	Lemon juice
3 T	Garlic, minced
2 t	Dijon mustard
2 t	Worcestershire sauce
16 oz	Fettuccine pasta
½ c	Italian flat-leaf parsley, finely chopped
2 lg	Lemon slices for serving.

Chicken Scallopini 🐤

30-35 minutes   **4 servings**

INGREDIENTS:

1 lb.	Linguine pasta
1 T	Olive oil
2 T	Butter
4	Chicken breasts
2 c	Panko

Lemon-butter sauce:

2 oz	Lemon juice
¼ c	Chicken broth
½ c	Heavy whipping cream
½ c	Butter, cubed
¼ t	Salt
¼ t	Pepper
3 T	Garlic, minced
1/3 c	Italian flat parsley, chopped
½ c	Dry white wine
¼ c	Capers
1/3 c	Parsley, finely chopped
	Lemon slices for serving

Directions:

Cook pasta according to package instructions, until al dente, and set aside.   Butterfly chicken, (slice horizontally) and use a meat mallet or heavy rolling pin to pound chicken

until it is about 1/4 inch thick. Salt and pepper chicken generously. Coat chicken with panko. Heat olive oil in a large skillet over medium-high heat. Sauté chicken until browned (about 3-4 minutes per side) then turn heat down to medium for another 2-3 minutes so it is cooked through, a total of 5 minutes per side. You want the outside brown without over cooking the inside. Transfer chicken to a separate plate. In the same skillet, heat

lemon juice, garlic, drained and rinsed capers over medium-high, bringing to a boil. Add wine and cook for 2 minutes. Add chicken broth and parsley, reduce the heat to medium-low for 2 minutes. Add cream slowly while stirring, until thickened, about 2-3 minutes. Add pine nuts. Add butter a few cubes at a time, slowly stirring until incorporated.

Add pasta to sauce and season with salt and pepper. Place chicken on top of pasta and garnish with lemon slices and serve!

(This receipt is great for veal scallopini.)

"Let's have a Party!"
Italian Casserole

1 hour, 20 minutes   It serves Eight!   And it's Great!

INGREDIENTS:	
2 lbs	Ground beef
1 lg	Onion, chopped
2 T	Garlic, minced
24 oz	Spaghetti sauce
14.5 oz	Canned diced tomatoes, undrained
4 oz	Canned mushrooms, drained
1 t	Italian seasoning
3c	Pasta shells
3	Plum tomatoes
¾ C	Provolone cheese, shredded
¾ C	Mozzarella cheese, shredded

Directions:

Preheat oven to 350°. In a large skillet, cook beef and onion over medium heat until beef is no longer pink, about 6-8 minutes. Add salt and pepper. Add garlic and cook until fragrant, about 1 minute. Drain grease from skillet. Stir in spaghetti sauce, diced tomatoes, mushrooms, and Italian seasoning and bring to a boil. Reduce heat to low and simmer, uncovered, for 20 minutes. Cook pasta until al dente. Drain pasta and add to beef mixture. Transfer the mixture to an ungreased 9x13-inch aluminum pan. Top with provolone and mozzarella cheese and bake until bubbly and heated through, about 30 minutes. Serve warm.

Add a salad and it's dinner for friends

Italian Pesto for Lovers

20 Minutes   4 Servings

Directions:

Combine all ingredients in food processor or blender and blend until coarsely combined or smooth depending on preference. I like to add the pine nuts last so I can control how coarse I want the pesto. I generally prefer to smooth pesto, but chunky/coarser is great too. Stop 3-4 times to scrape sides with spatula.

Transfer to small glass bowl with a lid or canning jar. Top with ½ inch olive oil and chill. The olive oil on top prevents browning of basil when it stays stored in the fridge. Great for a quick recipe.

Use pesto sauce with penne, linguini, or any other pasta and meatballs.

INGREDIENTS:

2T	Pine nuts
1 t	Salt
1 T	Garlic, minced
2c	Sweet Italian basil
½ c	Olive oil (add as needed if consistency is too thick)
½ c	Parmigiano-Reggiano, grated
¼ c	Pecorino Romano, grated

"Grandpa Roy's Famous"
Linguini Alla Vongole

INGREDIENTS:	
4 T	Olive Oil
4 T	Butter
3	Shallots, finely chopped
3 T	Garlic, minced
1 T	Basil
½ c	Dry White Wine
40 oz	½ Chopped and ½ minced canned clams
1 lb.	Linguine
1 c	Fresh Parsley finely chopped
16	Medium Shrimp
4 oz	Italian Pancetta
4 T	Pine nuts
	Salt and pepper to taste
	Romano Cheese to taste, shredded

45 minutes   4 servings

Directions:

In a small frying pan, sauté pancetta until crisp and set aside. Devein shrimp and set aside. In the grease created by the pancetta toast the pine nuts. (Watch closely, stir constantly, and don't burn.) In a large skillet, heat butter and olive oil over low heat. Add shallots, garlic and basil, sauté until tender. Turn heat to medium-high and add wine. Allow to cook for 2 minutes. Add parsley and clams with juice. Cook at medium until heated through.

Boil linguine until al dente, about 15 minutes. Add pine nuts, pancetta, and shrimp to clam sauce. Be careful not to overcook shrimp, about 1 to 2 minutes turning as you watch. Add linguine to sauce, a little pasta water to create extra sauce. Allow to cook on low for linguine to marinate in sauce. Top with shredded Romano cheese to taste.

This is a great appetizer dip for small pieces of French bread. (While cooking the linguine; in a small bowl, mix olive oil, Balsamic vinegar, ground pepper, basil, parsley, garlic, and graded cheese.)

"Heavenly"

Chicken Alfredo

30 minutes   **4 servings**

Directions:

In a large skillet heat oil over medium heat. Generously salt and pepper chicken. Sauté chicken until golden brown, about 7-8 minutes per side. Boil the fettuccini for 7 minutes and set aside (Pasta will finish cooking in sauce). To the same skillet add broth, milk, garlic, season with salt and pepper. Bring to a simmer, add fettuccine, and cook stirring frequently, until well combined, about 3 minutes. Continue to cook, tossing occasionally, until pasta is al dente, about 9 minutes more. Stir in Parmesan cheese and cream until combined. Simmer until sauce thickens, about 3-4 minutes. Remove from heat and mix in chicken. Top with parsley and serve.

INGREDIENTS:	
2 T	Olive oil
2	Chicken breasts
1 ½ c	Chicken broth
1 ½ c	Whole milk
1 T	Garlic, minced
8 oz	Fettuccine
1 c	Parmesan cheese, grated
½ c	Heavy cream
½ c	Parsley
	Kosher salt to taste
	Black pepper to taste

Champagne Chicken

1 hour   4 servings

This recipe features thinly sliced pieces of pan-fried chicken breast and mushrooms in a reduced wine sauce.

INGREDIENTS:	
4 T	Vegetable oil
3 T	Flour
1 t	Paprika
3 t	Tarragon (finely crumbled)
2 T	Garlic Butter
16	Mushrooms (medium sliced)
4	Chicken breasts
1 c	Champagne
1 c	Half and half
20	Cherry tomatoes
	Salt and pepper to taste

Directions:

Mix flour, paprika, salt, pepper, and tarragon, sprinkle on chicken. Sauté chicken in oil until brown (about 3 minutes per side on medium-high heat). Don't overcook, chicken will finish cooking after you add champagne. Add champagne to chicken and simmer with skillet partially covered until liquid is reduced by 50%. In a separate large skillet melt butter, add garlic, and sauté mushrooms and tomatoes about 4-5 minutes. Add tomatoes and mushrooms to chicken and place on a serving platter in oven at 200° to keep warm. Add heavy cream to sauce and stir on low-medium heat till slightly thickened. Pour sauce over warm chicken and tomatoes. Garnish a sprig or two of parsley.

"See You in My Dreams"
Fettuccine

40 minutes   **4 servings**

Directions:

Preheat oven to 375°. In a large oven-safe skillet over medium-high heat, heat oil. Generously, salt and pepper chicken. Sauté chicken until golden brown, about 4-5 minutes per side. Transfer to a plate and remove half of the grease from skillet. Cook fettuccine for 7 minutes and set aside. Over medium heat, cook garlic, thyme, and red pepper, stirring occasionally, until fragrant, about 1-2 minutes. Stir in broth, tomatoes, cream, and Parmesan cheese and season with salt. Bring to simmer, then return chicken to skillet. Transfer skillet to oven and bake until chicken is cooked through, about 10-12 minutes. A thermometer inserted in thickest part should read 165°. Add to fettuccine, top with basil and serve.

INGREDIENTS:	
1 T	Olive oil
4	Chicken breasts
3/4 c	Chicken broth
1 t	Red pepper flakes
1 T	Thyme leaves, fresh
½ c	Sun-dried tomatoes, chopped
1 T	Garlic, minced
8 oz.	Fettuccine
1/4 c	Parmesan cheese, grated
½ c	Heavy cream
½ c	Basil, fresh, torn in small pieces
	Kosher salt and black pepper to taste

I believe dreaming is important to a wonderful lifestyle as is expressed in my grandfather's poem. . .

 **Dream**

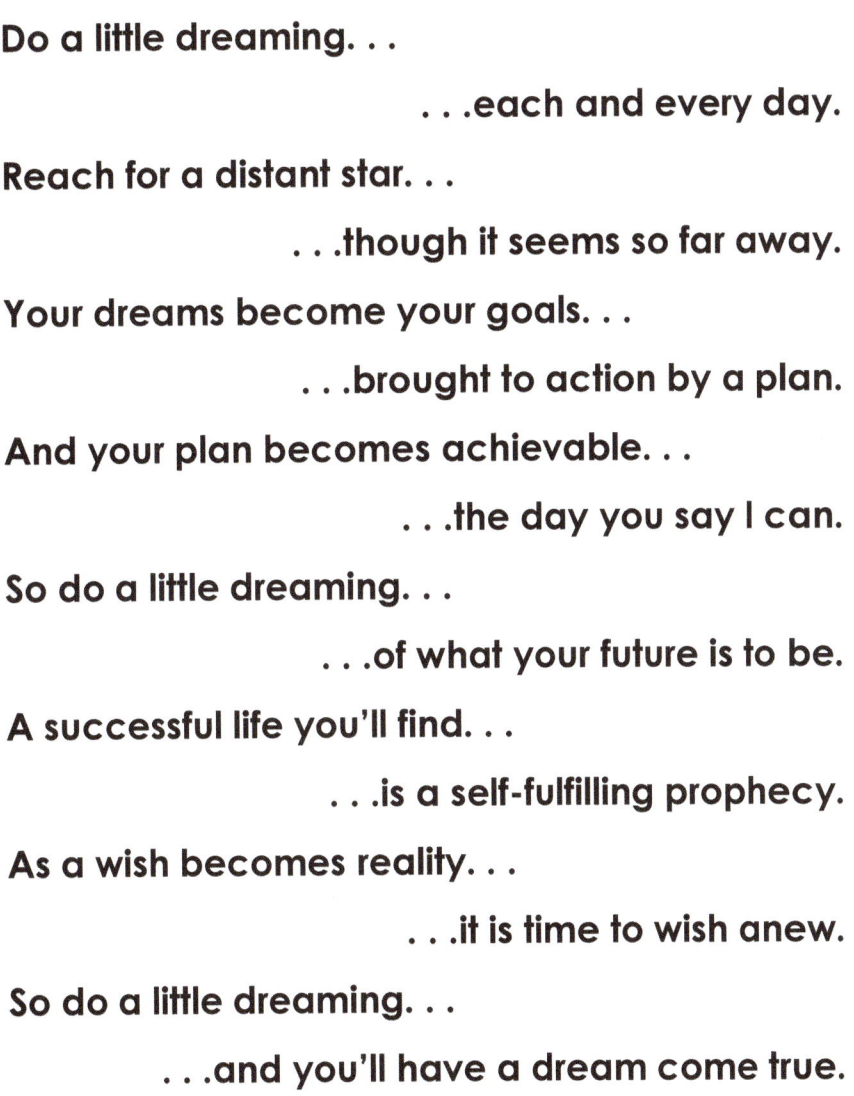

Do a little dreaming. . .

> . . .each and every day.

Reach for a distant star. . .

> . . .though it seems so far away.

Your dreams become your goals. . .

> . . .brought to action by a plan.

And your plan becomes achievable. . .

> . . .the day you say I can.

So do a little dreaming. . .

> . . .of what your future is to be.

A successful life you'll find. . .

> . . .is a self-fulfilling prophecy.

As a wish becomes reality. . .

> . . .it is time to wish anew.

So do a little dreaming. . .

> . . .and you'll have a dream come true.

RoyBain©1980

"Serve Me Hot Rigatoni"

1 Hour, 10 minutes   4 Servings

Directions:

Place olive oil in a small frying pan over medium-heat and sauté onion and salt for 5 minutes. Stir in garlic for one minute. Blend in tomatoes and water. Bring to a simmer; adjust to medium-low heat. Simmer stirring occasionally, for 45 t0 60 minutes. Reduce to low heat and add 2/3 basil to sauce. Stir in butter. When butter melts add cheese, 1/3 at a time. Cook rigatoni until al dente, boiled about 15 minutes and add to sauce. Sprinkle with remaining basil and graded cheese. Serve hot!

(Great with meatballs)

INGREDIENTS:	
4 T	Extra-virgin olive oil
8 oz	Rigatoni
1 c	Onion, diced
1 t	Salt
1 t	Red pepper flakes
3 T	Garlic cloves, minced
1-28 oz	Italian tomatoes, crushed
½ c	Water
4 T	Cold butter, cubed
½ c	Fresh basil leaves, thinly sliced
1 c	Parmigiano-Reggiano cheese, grated
	Salt and pepper, to taste

🏠 "Million Dollar"

Baked Ziti

INGREDIENTS:	
½ lb.	Sausage, ground
1	Medium onion
2 T	Garlic, minced
1	Carrot, finely diced
1 stick	Celery, finely diced
1 T	Tomato paste
1 t	Italian seasoning
1-14 oz	Jar of tomato basil sauce
½ c	Cream cheese, or ricotta
1 t	Salt and pepper
2-4 T	Pasta water
8 oz	Ziti
¼ c	Cooled pasta water
¾ c	Mozzarella cheese, shredded
¼ c	Parmesan cheese, grated

1 Hour   8 Servings

Directions:

Preheat oven to 350°. Boil Ziti (10 minutes) and hold. With a large, deep skillet over medium-high heat, cook sausage until brown, about 5-7 minutes. Add onion, garlic, carrot, celery, and cook until soften, about 5 minutes. Stir Italian seasoning and tomato paste into sausage mix. Add tomato/basil sauce to mixture. Simmer on low for 5 minutes. In medium bowl, stir the cream cheese, salt, pepper, and 2 to 4 tablespoons of pasta water together.

Layer in aluminum casserole pan.

Spread a layer of meat sauce on bottom of a 9x12 inch aluminum pan. Add ½ of pasta as second layer. Add 1/3 of mozzarella as third layer. Spread cream cheese mix on top of mozzarella as fourth layer. Add ½ of meat sauce as fifth layer. Add remaining pasta as sixth layer. Sprinkle 1/3 mozzarella as seventh layer. Top with remaining meat sauce as eighth layer. Sprinkle with mozzarella and parmesan and bake 25- 30 minutes. Serve HOT!

Garlic Goddess Pasta

30 minutes   **4 Servings**

Easy and you only use one pan!

INGREDIENTS:

2 t	Olive oil
4 T	Garlic, minced
4 c	Chicken broth
¼ t	Salt
½ t	Black pepper
½ lb	Spaghetti
¾ c	Parmesan cheese, grated
¾ c	Heavy cream
4 t	Parsley, chopped

Directions:

In a medium pan heat olive oil over medium heat. Add garlic and stir until fragrant, about 2 minutes. Add butter and stir until melted. Add chicken broth, salt, and pepper. Bring to a boil, add spaghetti, and cook until al dente, about 12 to 15 minutes. Add parmesan cheese, heavy cream, and parsley, stir until combined. Serve hot!

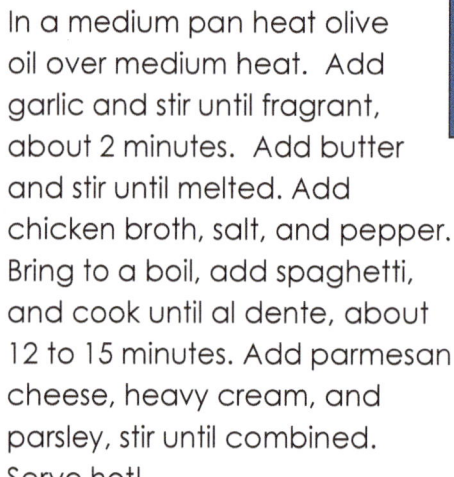

"Crazy-good"

 Garlic Kiscuits

30 minutes   **12 rolls**

INGREDIENTS:	
½ c	Unsalted butter, melted
1 T	Parmesan cheese, grated
2 T	Garlic, minced
½ t	Oregano, dried
½ t	Basil, dried
½ t	Parsley flakes, dried
	Salt to taste
1 tube	Refrigerated buttermilk biscuits

Directions:

In a large bowl, whisk together the melted butter, parmesan cheese, garlic, oregano, basil, parsley, and salt. Reserve 2 tablespoons of mixture. Cut each biscuit into six pieces. One-by-one press each kiscuit piece into the mix and place 4 or 5 pieces around in a circle and 1 piece in the center of the muffin tin. Bake the kiscuits pieces at 375° until they are golden brown, about 10-15 minutes. After browning brush each roll with the remaining mixture and serve.

"Home-made"

 *Happy Buns*

<table>
<tr><th colspan="2">INGREDIENTS:</th></tr>
<tr><td>1¼ c</td><td>Whole milk, warmed to room temperature.</td></tr>
<tr><td>1</td><td>Packet active dry yeast</td></tr>
<tr><td>2 T</td><td>Sugar</td></tr>
<tr><td>¼ c</td><td>Unsalted butter</td></tr>
<tr><td>1 lg.</td><td>Egg</td></tr>
<tr><td>1 t</td><td>Kosher salt</td></tr>
<tr><td>4 c</td><td>All-purpose flour</td></tr>
<tr><td>2 T</td><td>Unsalted butter, melted and mixed with 1 T honey.</td></tr>
</table>

2 hours   15 rolls

Directions:

Combine the milk, yeast, sugar in a small bowl and let stand until foamy, about 5 minutes. In the bowl of an electric mixer, using a dough hook attachment, beat the milk mixture with  the butter, egg, and two cups of flour on medium-low speed until a smooth batter forms, about 1-2 minutes. Gradually add the remaining 2 cups of flour with salt mixed in, ½ cup at a time, until a soft, smooth ball of dough forms. The dough should feel elastic and tacky to the touch. Increase the mixer speed to medium-high and mix for 3 minutes. Place the dough in a bowl that has been lightly coated with oil, turning the bowl to coat the dough. Cover the bowl with a clean towel and let it stand in a warm spot until the dough doubles in size, about 1 hour. Gently deflate the dough by punching it down. Using a rolling pin, working on a lightly floured surface, roll the dough into a ½-inch thick. Cut the dough into 15 squares. Fold the 4 corners of each square into the center, cupping the top of the square in the palm of your hand, forming the round top. Put the bottom of each roll where the 4 corners meet on the flat surface, slide it around giving it a flat smooth bottom.

 Preheat the oven to 375°. Place the rolls onto 1 or 2 baking sheets, cover with a clean towel and let stand in a warm spot until the dough has doubled in size, about 30-45 minutes. Place the baking sheets into the oven and bake until golden brown, about 14-16 minutes. Brush with butter and serve warm.

"Honey Gazed"

 # Carrots

"This **honey glazed carrots** recipe turns an easy everyday carrot into a show-stopping sweet and savory side dish."

20 minutes   4 servings

INGREDIENTS:

A touch of dried **rosemary** gives sweet, glazed carrots some herbal depth.

1½ lbs.	Carrots, peeled and cut into 2-inch lengths, halved, or quartered if thick.
4 T	Butter
4 T	Honey
3 T	Light-brown sugar
¼ t	Rosemary
¼ c	Parsley
	Kosher salt to taste
	Black pepper to taste

Directions:

In a large skillet, place carrots, and 1 1/4 cups water. Bring to a boil; reduce to a simmer, and cook until carrots are tender, 10 to 12 minutes. (If water evaporates before carrots are tender, add 1/4 cup more.) Drain and set aside. In the same skillet over medium-low heat, add butter, sugar, honey, rosemary, parsley and season with salt and pepper. Cook until sugar is dissolved. Stir in carrots and continue to cook, stirring frequently, until liquid is reduced to a glaze, 1 to 2 minutes more.

Serve Hot!

"Tender Sweet"
Baby Beets

30 minutes   **3-4 servings**

INGREDIENTS:

3-4	Baby Beets
	Butter
	Salt and pepper to taste

Directions:

Baby beets are best! Remove the tops leaving about two inches of tops. Place the beets in a small pot of waterand boil over medium heat until done. They should fall off a knife when pierced. Move to sink, cut off tops and roots, hold under cold water, squeeze and the peel will pop off. Add salt, pepper, and butter then serve.

Strawberry Delight

1 Hour 15 minutes   10 servings

INGREDIENTS:	
2 lbs.	Strawberries, halved
¾ c	Powdered sugar
1 T	Lemon juice
¼ t	Kosher salt
¼ t	Vanilla extract
?	Vanilla ice cream

Directions:

Preset oven to 400°. In a large bowl, gently stir together strawberries, powdered sugar, lemon juice, and salt. Spoon the strawberry mixture into a 9x13-inch baking pan. Bake for 25 to 30 minutes, stir after 15 minutes. Remove from oven and stir in vanilla extract. Allow them to rest for 30 minutes and serve warm over ice cream!

"Blow Your Mind"
Cherries Jubilee

30 minutes   6 servings

INGREDIENTS:

½ c	Sugar
2 T	Cornstarch
¼ c	Cold water
¼ c	Orange juice
1 lb.	Dark Cherries, pitted
½ t	Orange zest, finely grated
¼ t	Cherry extract
¼ c	Brandy
	Vanilla ice cream

Directions:

Whisk sugar and cornstarch together in a wide saucepan. Stir in water and orange juice; bring to a boil over medium-high heat, whisking until thickened. Stir in cherries and orange zest; return to a boil, then reduce heat, and simmer for 10 minutes. While cherries are cooking, spoon ice cream into serving bowls.

Remove cherries from heat and stir in cherry extract. Pour in brandy and ignite with a long lighter. Gently shake the pan until blue flame has extinguished itself. Spoon cherries over ice cream.

Note on flambéing:

The flames may get quite high when flambéing, so pay attention to anything flammable above and around where you ignite the cherries. When the initial large flame has died down, a small blue flame will continue to burn for several seconds. Shake or stir the cherries gently to expose more alcohol to the flame, being careful that they do not burn. The goal is to have the small, blue flame burn for as long as possible, thereby reducing the raw alcohol flavor, caramelizing the sugars, and entertaining your guests!

Haley's Recipe for a fantastic lifestyle

3 cup of pleasant thoughts

1 cup of kind deeds

1 cup of consideration for others

2 cups of forgiveness

3 cups of well-planned goals

Mix thoroughly and add an

abundance of happiness and serve with a smile.

And . . .

"Put a little LOVE in all you do!"

Love

God gives to thee an abundance of love

through friends and family, from heaven above.

Try as you will, all of your love to give

you'll have plenty still, for as long as you live.

For love is to share, and not meant to store;

show others you care, and you'll always have more.

God did not place love in your heart to stay;

for love is not love, until you give it away.

Roy Bain © 1981